Basher Science

GREEN TECHNOLOGY

KINGFISHER
LONDON & NEW YORK

T0011397

KINGFISHER
LONDON & NEW YORK

First published 2022 in the United States by Kingfisher
120 Broadway, New York, NY 10271
Kingfisher is an imprint of Macmillan Children's Books, London
All rights reserved.

Author: Tom Jackson
Consultant: Michael Craig
Editor: Anna Southgate
Designer: Dave Jones
Proofreader: Richard Beatty

Dedicated to Hanna Elvinsson-Irish

Distributed in the U.S. and Canada by Macmillan,
120 Broadway, New York, NY 10271

EU representative: 1st Floor, The Liffey Trust Centre,
117-126 Sheriff Street Upper, Dublin 1 D01 YC43

Library of Congress Cataloging-in-Publication Data has been applied for.

ISBN: 978-0-7534-7814-1 (Hardcover)
ISBN: 978-0-7534-7815-8 (Paperback)

Kingfisher books are available for special promotions and premiums.
For details contact: Special Markets Department, Macmillan, 120 Broadway,
New York, NY 10271

For more information, please visit www.kingfisherbooks.com

Printed in China
9 8 7 6 5 4 3 2 1
1TR/0122/WKT/RV/128MA

CONTENTS

Introduction   4

Team Now   6

Fab Futurists   28

Pollution Police   52

Glossary   62

Index   64

Introduction
Sustainability

What's tech? And why's it even green? Good questions, and it's up to me to explain. I'm Sustainability—I give, but I will never take away, and this book is all about me. Tech (short for technology) means any clever gizmo invented to do something useful. But *green* tech describes an invention that does its job without causing damage to Nature, so the environment can stay healthy and green.

Green tech does its job sustainably. That means it uses renewable resources—things like light, wind, and heat that will never run out because Nature constantly replaces or renews them. Better still, green tech makes far less pollution. This is anything made by humans that builds up and causes problems for the planet. Take plastic, for example, which hangs around in soil and sea for centuries. Or what about greenhouse gases in the air, such as carbon dioxide? They might be invisible, but they are storing up climate troubles for everyone. Making the most of my sustainable ways, green tech is important for slowing climate change and reducing environmental damage. One day, I am sure, all tech will be green tech.

Chapter 1
Team Now

Hey, we are here already, working hard to save the planet! Our biggest job is cleaning up power production. For too long, technology has relied on dirty fossil fuels such as coal, natural gas, and oil to make electricity and drive engines. These fuels create a lot of pollution, which has been left to mix up with fresh air, clean water, and fertile soil for years and years. We say stop that right now! We can keep the lights on without damaging the climate, and power cars and heat homes while keeping the air smoke free. Look around for us—we're becoming much more common.

Solar
Panel

Concentrated
Solar

Wind
Turbine

Geothermal
Power

Nuclear
Energy

Fuel Cell

Biofuel

Hydro-
electricity

Pumped
Storage

Electric
Car

Rewilding

Solar Panel
Team Now

☀ The shining star of pollution-free power
☀ Uses chemical know-how to switch sunbeams to sparks
☀ Can be used in large numbers to make a solar farm

I am a flat and flashy slab of power that turns sunlight directly into all-zinging, all-zapping electricity. Arguably one of the most valuable Team Now players, I'm the bright spark leading the way to your low-pollution future. I don't need flames or fuels, smoke or fire to create a useful supply of power. Just a sunny day will do.

Clever chemicals in my top layer perform an almost magical trick called the "photovoltaic effect." It switches a light beam's energy into an electric current that's no different from currents made in fossil-fuel-driven power plants. Solar farms are springing up in sunbaked spots, where I line up in my hundreds and thousands to catch some rays. I'll work almost anywhere—expect to see me on a building near you soon. Don't say so long, say solar.

● A day's sunlight holds 10,000 times the energy used by humans in that time
● Just 3% of the electricity we use per year is made using solar power
● Scientists are developing photovoltaic paint to turn walls into solar panels

Solar Panel

Concentrated Solar

Team Now

☀ This focused fellow is powered by the Sun's heat
☀ Goes with the flow to save on pollution and money
☀ Converts heat into electricity without burning anything at all

The Sun is really hot stuff—nothing new there—but did you know that I can harness that heat? At my simplest, I'm a panel of water pipes on a house roof or sunny wall. Dark in color (to absorb more light and heat), I provide hot water for showers and baths that is green, clean, and free!

I can also scale up to make clean power. Like my close cousin Solar Panel, you'll most likely see me putting searing sunbeams to good use in deserts. In this mode, I form a row of curved panels lined with mirrors. My curves focus the hot, hot sunbeams onto a long slender tube of water. Inside the tube, the water fizzes into a blast of supersquashed steam bursting to get out. I'll use that hot steam to drive generators, just like old-school power plants do. Stay cool—my hot tech is here to help.

● The concentrated solar system was invented in 1886
● The first concentrated solar power plant was built in Egypt in 1913
● The largest concentrated solar power plant, in California, has 173,500 mirrors

Concentrated Solar

Wind Turbine
Team Now

* This great rotator is a stand-up power player
* Uses a flow of wind to make a flow of electricity
* Appearing at a wind farm near you

When the breezes start to blow, they put me in a spin. I'm a new-fashioned windmill, but instead of grinding grain, I churn out clean electricity. My long, wing-shaped blades work like a giant fan in reverse. Instead of pushing out a cooling blast as they slice through the air, they catch the natural flow of the wind, which makes them rotate even faster. A generator in my central hub uses that rotation to create an electric current.

I've been around as an idea for hundreds of years, getting bigger and better all the time. The question is where to put me. I need a place with strong, smooth winds. Hilltops are good, but some say I spoil the view. On most land areas the wind is too stop-and-start. I like it best out at sea, where wind farms are sprouting like iron forests.

- The largest wind turbines are almost as tall as the Eiffel Tower
- The world's biggest farm is in northern China and has 7,000 turbines
- About 6% of the world's electricity needs are provided by wind power

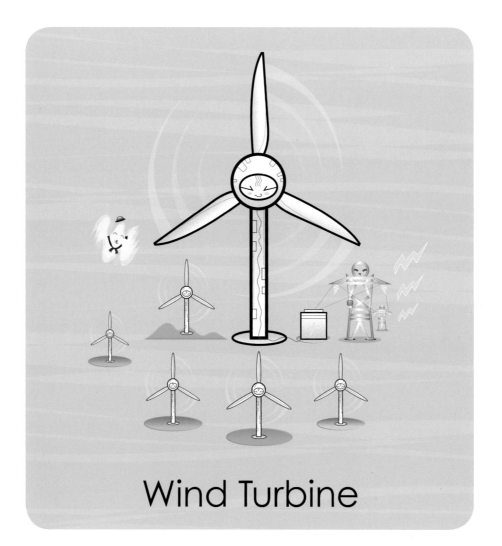

Wind Turbine

Geothermal Power
Team Now

* This power player loops in to the heat beneath the ground
* A simple system that works by volcanic action
* Geothermal is a scientific word for "heat of Earth"

The big thing about green tech is that it works hand in hand with Earth, and I get closer than most by giving the planet a warm hug. Deep beneath your feet, solid rocks give way to megahot magma. In areas with volcanoes, this seething gloop comes close enough to the surface for me to reach down and collect some of its heat.

I send pipes down into the hot zone, choosing rocks that are soaked with hot water. In one pipe, I pump up some of that hot stuff, hissing with steam. As I do, I push down some cold water in another pipe to replace the hot water I'm taking. The rock-heated water and steam bursts up to the surface, straight into my powerhouse, where I turn the fast blast into electricity. Any hot water left over (often plenty) is sent to heat nearby houses or even cities!

* The first geothermal system, built in Italy in 1904, powered four light bulbs
* Iceland makes almost all of its electricity using geothermal power
* Geothermal pipes go 1.8 mi. (3 km) deep; in the future they could go deeper

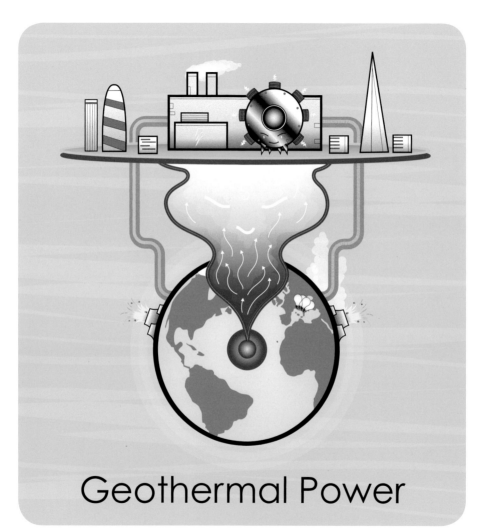

Geothermal Power

Nuclear Energy
Team Now

* ✳ This power supply makes heat using radioactive metals
* ✳ Can be dirty and dangerous, but also kind to the climate
* ✳ Makes electricity without leaking out greenhouse gases

Do I have a place in this clean, green team? You betcha! I make electricity (lots of it) using nuclear fuel. It is true that I give out harmful radioactive rays as well as useful heat, *and* that it will take a very long time to make my waste safe. But who else can work day and night to supply as much power as I can without damaging the climate? No one, that's who.

Nuclear Energy

* ● Building a huge nuclear power plant releases a lot of carbon dioxide (CO_2)
* ● But once a nuclear power plant is up and running, it releases very little CO_2
* ● Radioactive waste must be stored safely for thousands of years

Fuel Cell
Team Now

* A superclean chemical-fueled power supply
* This sparky unit uses eco-friendly fuels to make electricity
* Puffs out steam to create pollution-free power

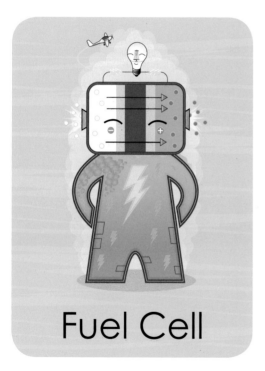

Fuel Cell

Half like an engine, half like a battery, I'm all green. Like a battery, I produce electricity by making two chemicals react. Unlike a battery, those chemicals never run out but are pumped into me like engine fuel. At my simplest, I work using oxygen and hydrogen gas. The two fuels combine to make electricity and an exhaust gas that is nothing but clean steam, pure and simple.

- The fuel cell was invented by Welsh scientist William Grove in 1838
- The first aircraft to be powered by a fuel cell was flown in 2003
- One fuel cell design uses chemicals made by tiny green algae living inside it

Biofuel
■ Team Now

✴ Fuel that grows on trees, in fields, and in you!
✴ A clean system that uses plant and animal remains
✴ AKA biodiesel, biogas, and biocoal

Why use fusty old fossil fuels when you can grow your own? I'm fuel made from waste food, wood, or even poop! Fossil fuels are rich in carbon, which burns nicely and gives off a big bang of heat. But the flaming fuel turns into carbon dioxide (and other things), which upsets the delicate balance of our climate.

Now come and see what I can do. Plants take carbon dioxide out of the air, and a few million years later the fossil remains of life-forms are oil, coal, and natural gas. Well, I use my tech to short-circuit that cycle and make faster fuels from the remains of life. Sugar becomes a liquid fuel that works just like gasoline. I make gas from waste foods and turn poop into charcoal. The idea is that I won't add extra carbon to the air as I burn—I just put back what I took out.

● Using human poop to make fuel could provide power for 138 million homes
● In the United States, most gasoline for cars already contains 10% biofuel
● Biofuels can cause big problems if wild forests are cleared to grow them

Biofuel

Hydroelectricity
■ Team Now

* ☀ A wet and wild power source that takes on entire rivers
* ☀ Tames the flow of water and puts it to work
* ☀ Uses immense dams to control rivers

"The river flows, it flows to the sea. Where that river goes, that's where I want to be." That's a song about me! The hydro in my name stands for "water." Instead of wind or hot steam, I use the thunderous flow of a river to make electricity. I take control and make the river do some hard work as it flows.

First, I need a dam—a giant wall thrown bank-to-bank across a river. This controls the flow of the water and creates a deep and sleepy lake upstream. The water funnels through tight tunnels in my dam. Before it reaches the other side, the roaring rapids run into huge bucket-like turbines. These are mechanical devices that spin around and around. As they do so, they turn generators that create another kind of flow—the flow of electricity.

* Three Gorges Dam in China is the world's largest hydroelectric power plant
* Switzerland produces 88% of its power via hydroelectricity
* The first hydroelectricity system was built in 1878 in England; it powered one light

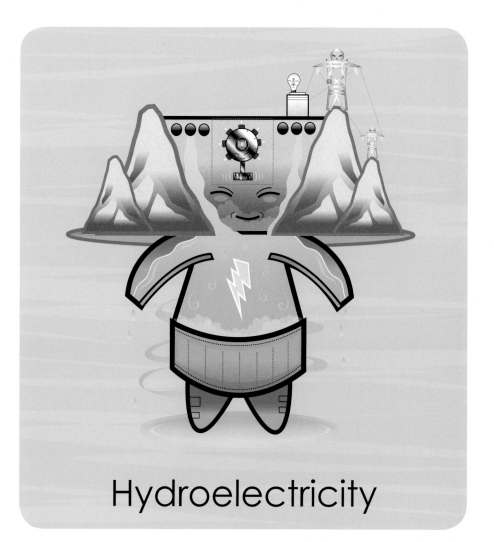

Hydroelectricity

Pumped Storage
Team Now

* ☀ This pumped-up type stores unused electricity
* ☀ Uses hydroelectricity to make electricity on demand
* ☀ Water goes uphill to save power for later

When the Sun blazes, the winds blow, and the rivers flow, Team Now churns out more power than is needed. But the opposite happens, too. Solar Panel switches off at night, Wind Turbine winds down when the breeze drops, and Hydroelectricity can be left high and dry in the summer, when river levels fall. Don't worry—I'll keep the lights on.

I hang out in steep mountains because I need two lakes, or basins, one high above the other. In times of plenty, I use spare power to make a reverse waterfall, pumping water uphill from my lower basin to my upper one. When it is time for a power boost, I let the water flush back down again, directing it through my generator, which turns all that stored energy back into useful electricity. What goes up must come down—I'm feeling pumped!

* ● The world's pumped storage plants hold 9,000 gigawatts
* ● 9,000 gigawatts is enough to power all of Bolivia for a year
* ● The first pumped storage plant was built in Switzerland in 1907

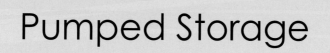

Pumped Storage

Electric Car
Team Now

☀ An all-electric road warrior ready for a green revolution
☀ This zippy ride produces no pollution as it drives
☀ Just needs a plug to keep the show on the road

Honk, honk! You might not notice me, because I look just like a gasoline-powered car (although I'm often much quieter). I have neither engine nor fuel tank, but an electric motor and a big battery. Instead of refueling after a long trip, I like to plug in to a high-powered electricity supply and recharge. Eat sparks, gas-guzzlers!

I know what you are thinking: I'm really cool—but am I very green? Well, I don't produce choking fumes, which is a bonus, but to be of real benefit I need to get my electric power from a member of Team Now. If I'm charged using current made by a dirty burner, such as coal, oil, or natural gas, I'm still part of the problem. Pretty soon all new cars and trucks will be like me, and that will help drive the Green Tech Revolution. Let's roll!

● Electric cars are actually old tech—the first was built in 1890!
● The fastest electric car is the Buckeye Bullet. It can go 341 mph (549 kmh)
● Formula E is an international racing series for electric cars

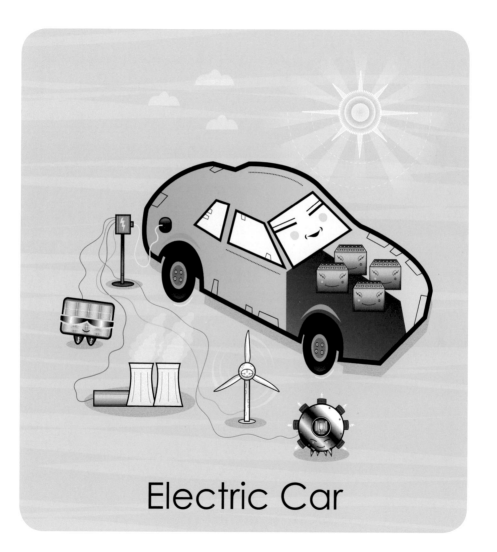

Electric Car

Rewilding
■ Team Now

☀ A supersimple tree-planting system with awesome outcomes
☀ Fixes the climate by returning the land to wilderness
☀ Uses nature to rebalance the gases in the atmosphere

Sure, I get it—new things are exciting, and that goes for Green Tech, too. But old things (like me) can be just as important. Am I even a type of technology? We can talk about that, but there is no discussion over how helpful I am in the fight against climate change.

To get me going, just plant some trees. There are billions of you out there, so what are you waiting for? I'd love to see more wilderness in the world. The trees and other plants (and the bodies of animals and fungi living in and around them) will soak up the extra carbon dioxide in the air. This is what it's all about, remember? The hard part is choosing which pieces of land go back to the wild, and which places are needed by you guys for farms and cities. Join me and you will be making your world much greener—literally.

● Experts have calculated there is room for 1.2 trillion new trees on Earth
● If we all planted 150 trees, extra carbon dioxide in the air would be cut by 75%
● Britain was once 90% forest; today forest covers just 13%, but that figure is rising

Rewilding

Chapter 2
Fab Futurists

We're a bunch of newbies, a set of supersmart ideas and tech-tastic inventions looking to change the future. Some of us will be more successful than others, sure, but we're all willing to give it a go. Who's your top pick? Is it Carbon Capture, who has the task of cleaning up the air, or perhaps Nuclear Fusion, who'll be making unlimited electricity using the power of a star? Maybe one day you'll sit back on a Hyperloop ride past the Energy Vault and wonder what all the fuss was about? Here's to that fabulous future!

Tidal Lagoon

Power Tower

Thermovoltaics

Storage Battery

Smart Grid

Air Energy Storage

Energy Vault

Vertical Farm

Artificial Photosynthesis

Nuclear Fusion

Hyperloop

Spaceplane

Telepresence Robot

Carbon Capture

Geoengineering

Tidal Lagoon
Fab Futurists

* Salty surf dude that grabs hold of the surging tides
* A massive tank out at sea that collects rising waters
* Water moving in and out is converted to electricity

Tides run like clockwork. You can set your watch by them as the ocean surges up the shore and then washes away again, twice every day. All that moving water! What power, what energy! And it's all there for the taking.

An enormous structure built in shallow seas, I turn the tide's ups and downs into a clean stream of power. Here's how I operate. First, I wall off a round patch of seabed. The tide pushes its way in past my turbines, generating power as it goes. At high tide I'm all filled up, but guess what happens next? Yes! The tide goes out again, barging through those turbines once more. Thanks, more power for me. I'm simple, but very big and hugely expensive. There aren't very many of me around yet, but I'm hoping one day I'll get to help save the world.

- The world's tides contain 3 trillion watts, enough power for 1 billion people
- The world's first tidal lagoon is planned for the southern coast of Wales
- First tidal power plant: a dam built at the mouth of the Rance River, France (1960)

Tidal Lagoon

Power Tower
Fab Futurists

* A giant fellow, always focused on harnessing heat
* Uses concentrated sunshine to create high temperatures
* Replaces sooty steel furnaces and chemical reactors

Stand back, human! My insides are hotter than a lake of lava, and I have heat rays that can melt metal. No longer will chemical plants and steelmakers need filthy coal and other fossil fuels to fire up their furnaces. Instead, I can provide all the heat they will ever need, drawn from the awesome power of sunlight alone.

I am a towering figure surrounded by curved mirrors very like the ones Concentrated Solar uses. They track the Sun to make sure its beams are always reflected up toward my mighty head. That focused ray of sunshine hits 6,300°F (3,500°C), way hotter than a puny coal fire. Waste not, want not! When unused, the beam melts a salty mixture stored within me that will keep hold of all that heat until it is needed. Oooh, it makes me feel all warm inside!

* The world's largest solar furnace is a 178 ft. (54 m) power tower in Odeillo, France
* Tallest power tower: 861 ft. (262 m) tall; it is in Dubai and helps make electricity
* The hot beams kill birds and insects that fly through them

Power Tower

Thermovoltaics
Fab Futurists

☀ A warm type that turns heat into electricity
☀ Uses tech similar to Solar Panel to harness the Sun's heat
☀ The heat in sunshine holds more energy than the light

Did you know that there is clean energy coming from the Sun that is even more powerful than sunlight? Can you guess what it is? Getting warmer? The answer is infrared radiation (that's heat, to you). I work like Solar Panel, only I make electricity from heat instead of light. And here's the best part. I work at night because the air stays hot even after the Sun's gone down.

Thermo-voltaics

● Around 55% of sunlight is infrared; the rest is visible light and ultraviolet light (UV)
● Thermovoltaic panels can generate up to one-fourth of their power at night
● Thermovoltaic tiles are being developed for use on domestic rooftops

Storage Battery
Fab Futurists

※ Dependable power player with a long history
※ Soaks up the grid's unused electricity ready for a rainy day
※ Being installed in a home near you soon!

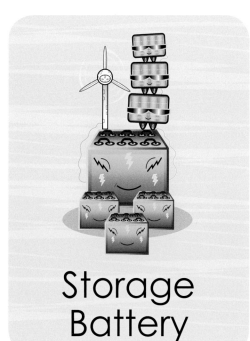

Storage Battery

I know! Weren't batteries invented, like, 100 years ago? It was 1800, actually, but I'm *rechargeable* now. In the future, giant versions of me will store spare electricity made by Solar Panel and Wind Turbine to prevent that clean power from going to waste. And when the Sun won't shine or the wind drops, I will step up to share my bounty. I'll keep your home powered up come rain or shine!

● Batteries use lithium, the lightest of all metals, to store electricity
● A gigafactory is the new name for a place that makes storage batteries
● California's largest battery storage station holds enough power to run 300 homes

Smart Grid
Fab Futurists

- ✳ A clever controller that keeps electricity flowing
- ✳ Uses artificial intelligence to manage the power supply
- ✳ Decides when to make power and when to store or use it

I'm a smart type who'll help you humans make the most of Team Now's sustainable power. Sure, Mother Nature has real control, but there are days when the Sun won't shine and the wind won't blow. What happens then? How will the Internet, hospitals, and cars keep on running?

Well, I will save the day with my fab plan to upgrade the old electricity grid. That system works by flowing electricity from where it is made (a fossil-fueled power plant) to where it is used (your home). But things are changing. Homes make use of Solar Panel now, while Storage Battery takes in and gives out power all the time. And me? I'm a master controller who uses artificial intelligence to direct green energy to the right place at the right time. Nothing gets wasted on my watch. Power to the people!

- ● The U.S. power grid aims to be made smart by the year 2030
- ● Grids already use smart meters to assess how much power a house is using
- ● Smart grids will store power in electric car batteries when they are not driving

Smart Grid

Air Energy Storage
Fab Futurists

✳ This big drip stores valuable power with a huff and a puff
✳ Uses spare electricity to compress air or chill it into liquid
✳ Releases a flow of air to be converted back into electricity

I'm a simple type, nothing but a puff of air, but I might become a future fix for power supply problems. We all love renewable energy, but it is not reliable. Sometimes you humans make too much, and other times too little.

Pumped Storage is already hard at work smoothing out supplies, but it needs a lot of water and a tall mountain to work well. In flat lands, I'll step up by saving unused electricity. I'm not much more than a tank of ultra-dry air. I use electric pumps to squish and squeeze the air into a tight bubble or to chill it into a supercool liquid. Then, when the times comes, I release the trapped air and let the liquid bubble and boil. That creates fast jets of gas that make turbines whiz around, creating a fresh supply of electricity in the process. I'm simple but effective.

● The first compressed air storage plant was built in Germany in 1978
● Liquified air is cooled to –319°F (–195°C)
● A cooled liquid air system planned for the U.S. will store energy for 100 houses

Air Energy Storage

Energy Vault
Fab Futurists

☀ A high-rise power storage system
☀ Uses spare energy to hoist blocks to the top of a tower
☀ Releases stored energy by dropping the blocks back down

Looking a little like a construction site, I'm a tower of heavy concrete blocks, stacked up like giant toy bricks. When there is spare power, Smart Grid directs my robotic electric cranes to hoist more blocks to the top. And when a power boost is needed, the top blocks drop back to the ground. Generators in my crane hoists spin as the blocks fall, turning those long drops into electricity.

Energy Vault

● The idea for an energy vault was only made public in 2017
● A 38.5-ton block holds the energy used to power five houses a day
● The first energy vault tower, built in Switzerland, is 360 ft. (110 m) tall

Vertical Farm
Fab Futurists

- ☀ A new food producer that reaches for the sky
- ☀ Protects wildlife by growing crops in high-rise fields
- ☀ Brings farming into the heart of the city

Vertical Farm

I'm a farming fix that makes heads turn. Regular farms use up wilderness areas, destroying wild habitats and wildlife. But I switch direction and go vertical, like a leafy high-rise. I'm stacked with racks for growing fruits and veggies. Water trickles down from roof tanks, and when the Sun sets, my bright lights keep the growing going. I'll even work in cities. With me, the sky's the limit.

- The largest vertical farm, in New Jersey, grows 9.5 tons of veggies a year
- A vertical tomato farm in Iceland uses heat from a volcano for winter growth
- Vegetables grow three times faster indoors than in an open field

Artificial Photosynthesis

Fab Futurists

* A chemical technology that aims to improve on nature
* Increases the efficiency of plant photosynthesis
* Could be a green way to make new fuels

Photosynthesis is a sun-powered process in which plants use red and blue light to make sugar. The green light just bounces off and is wasted. I'm a mix of advanced tech that aims to improve on nature to make plants use all light energy. I'll likely do this with modified microbes that photosynthesize to make not sugar but a clean fuel like hydrogen gas or flammable oil.

Artificial Photosynthesis

● Fuels made this way could be even more efficient than solar panels
● Natural photosynthesis uses only 6% of the energy in sunlight
● Artificial photosynthesis is more than 20% efficient

Nuclear Fusion

Fab Futurists

* This shining star could solve all our energy problems
* Re-creates the conditions inside a star
* Works by releasing energy from atoms

Nuclear Fusion

Stars like the Sun get hot because tiny atoms deep inside are smashed together very hard. The core, or nucleus, in each atom fuses, giving off a massive flash of energy. That fusion is me, and I promise unlimited clean power. But no one's managed to make me work yet on Earth. A huge fusion reactor is being built in France. That'll be my big chance to prove myself.

● A tokamak: an experimental, magnetic, doughnut-shaped fusion reactor
● ITER, the world's largest tokamak, is being built in France; it will be ready in 2025
● Fusion power is four million times more powerful than burning coal

Hyperloop
Fab Futurists

☀ Ground-based transportation system with the speed of a jet
☀ Uses a blast of air to push passenger cars though airless tubes
☀ Could replace air travel for making long trips

Am I a train? Am I an airplane? No, I'm Hyperloop, the next revolution in transportation. I can travel at the same speeds as a jetliner, but I don't leave the ground. Instead, my passenger cars whiz through long tube-like tunnels. But—get this—I have no wheels and not even a track!

So what's my trick? I'm in a very pressurized situation. My carriage fits tightly into the tube. In front of me the air is sucked out, making a near vacuum. Behind me comes a bullet of air shoving me forward, and off I go! Faster and faster. A cushion of air forms around my passenger cars so they float off the ground. There's no stopping me now. My tubes could one day crisscross the world and spell the end for smoke-spurting air travel. All aboard for a fast ride to the future!

● "Atmospheric railways" built in the 1840s used a simple version of this system
● The first human passengers tested a hyperloop in 2020
● India, Canada, the U.S., Poland, and South Korea all have hyperloop plans

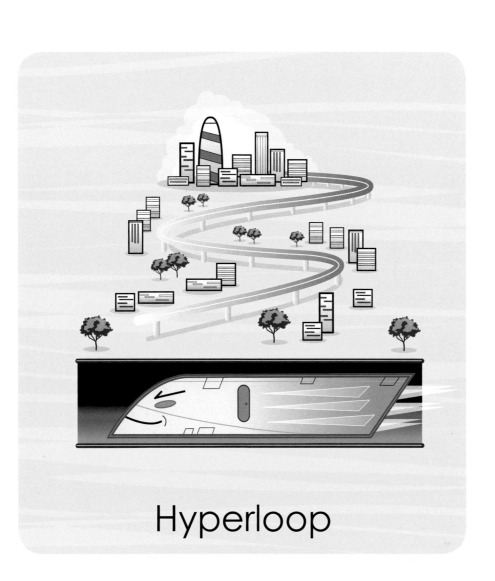

Hyperloop

Spaceplane
Fab Futurists

✳ This high-speed rocket plane runs on hydrogen fuel
✳ Makes travel faster, cheaper, and cleaner
✳ A superefficient way to reach space

This is where high tech meets green tech. I know, fuel-guzzling rocket planes do not seem green, but my design uses hydrogen. It burns into nothing but clean steam as it powers me to five times the speed of sound. In just four hours, you could be halfway around the world, pollution free. My engine, called SABRE, is half space rocket and half jet, and I work in space, too! I'll deliver, fast!

Spaceplane

● Skylon, the first spaceplane powered by SABRE, is planned for 2030
● A SABRE-powered flight from London to Sydney would take just over four hours
● The top speed of a SABRE engine in air is 3,943 mph (6,346 kmh)

Telepresence Robot
Fab Futurists

✳ Simple type that allows you to travel without leaving home
✳ A mash-up of video conferencing and robotics
✳ Gives you a physical presence in a far-off land

Telepresence Robot

Hello, I'm you! Well, I'm a robot version that you control from far away. I cut out long-distance travel and all the pollution it makes. At my simplest I'm a video screen on wheels, but I may get legs and arms in the future. You guide me around buildings and streets to attend meetings and visit friends. The people there can see you and talk via my screen. Enjoy your trip!

● Television means "seeing from afar"; telepresence means "being there from afar"
● The first telepresence robot was built by the U.S. Air Force in 1992
● A telepresence robot costs anywhere from $1,000 to $15,000

Carbon Capture
Fab Futurists

☀ A superhero sent to save the world. But will it work?
☀ Trialing a tech mixture to remove carbon dioxide from the air
☀ Hides away the unwanted carbon, rendering it harmless

It is my job to clean up this planet by scrubbing away carbon dioxide and other nasty climate-killing pollution from the air. Along with the computer, the light bulb, and the printing press, I could be one of those great inventions that change the world forever. But there is a lot riding on me to deliver a big win for green tech.

I have a lot of plans. I'm trying to use clever chemicals and filters to remove the carbon dioxide from the air or from the smoke made when fossil fuels burn. What then? Perhaps I can make the captured carbon into a fuel or rock, but most likely it will be my job to stash the carbon dioxide away to stop it from messing with the weather. One big idea is to pump all that unwanted gas underground into empty oil wells.

● Carbon dioxide makes up just 0.04% of the gases in the air
● Each year humans release 38.5 billion tons of extra carbon dioxide into the air
● Unwanted carbon dioxide was first pumped down into an oil well in 1972

Carbon Capture

Geoengineering
Fab Futurists

✸ A big thinker with planet-sized ideas
✸ Has many adventurous schemes for righting climate wrongs
✸ This risk taker could possibly make things even worse

The climate crisis is a big problem that needs a special engineer to fix it—a geoengineer like me with grand planet-wide schemes. Let's pump dust high into the sky from a fleet of solar-powered airships. The dust would reflect away sunlight to make Earth dimmer and cooler. Or why not squirt iron-rich sludge into the oceans using robotic tankers. The iron would help plankton grow, taking carbon dioxide out of the water. Or we could launch giant sunshades into space to chill Earth's climate.

What could possibly go wrong? Answer: a lot, and since some of my engineering projects are so huge that they would take decades to complete, we'd only know after it was too late. Perhaps my ideas are too big and too risky. Let's hope my Fab Futurist pals can do the job!

● 2 lb. (1 kg) of iron added to seawater could create 11 tons of plankton
● The cost of launching space shades has been estimated at $750 billion
● In 1991 the dust from a volcanic eruption caused a global cooling of 1°F (0.6°C)

Geoengineering

Chapter 3
Pollution Police

Seal off the area! We're here to stop pollution in its tracks. We wish there was nothing to see here, but pollution from plastics, smoke, and greenhouse gases has become a serious problem. We Green Techies are here to help, and we can clean up the problem, but you humans have an important role to play, too. You could start by cutting down on the things you use. Try buying less and repair and reuse stuff instead. When you absolutely have to throw something away, strip off everything that can be recycled first. Multiplied billions of times over, these tiny things will have a huge effect. Move along now!

Recycling
Machine

Biodegradable
Plastic

Ocean
Cleanup

Agrorobot

Waste
Incinerator

Catalytic
Converter

Recycling Machine
■ Pollution Police

❊ A mechanical megastar that reduces waste
❊ Uses clever tools to separate useful materials from litter
❊ Humans remove plastic bags, which might cause a jam

Watch that waste line! Don't you know that all those unwanted pieces of plastic, paper, glass, and metal can be used again? Let me help! With my fantastically long conveyor belt system and super sorting mechanisms, I'll have the use*ful* stripped from the use*less* in no time.

First, I'll filter out the big stuff, like cardboard and paper. They slide over gaps in my conveyor and a strong fan blows the paper out of the cardboard to separate them. Smaller stuff drops through to the belt below. Heavy glass and metal drop farther than the lighter plastics. I have lasers for detecting different kinds of plastic. They target jets of air to blast the useful types out of the mix! Then come magnets to pull out the iron objects and an electric field that swipes away aluminum, leaving just glass.

● The recycling center in Milpitas, California, sorts 110 tons of trash an hour
● Big recycling machines have conveyor belts that add up to 1.2 mi. (2 km)
● Germany recycles two-thirds of its waste—twice as much as the United States

Recycling Machine

Biodegradable Plastic
■ Pollution Police

☀ Self-destructing material that won't hang around
☀ Can be eaten away by bugs, unlike other kinds of plastic
☀ One way to reduce pollution on land and in the ocean

A new kind of material, I'm here to make regular plastic a thing of the past. All kinds of plastics (including me) copy natural substances like wood or skin. We are polymers, which means we are made from small units that are chained together to make strong sheets and long fibers. When natural polymers (wood, skin) come to the end of their usefulness, molds and germs chop them up into their simple ingredients. But these bugs can't handle most plastics, so those toughies stay around for years and years.

I'm different, because bacteria *can* break the links in my chains. Sure, it might take a few years, but once I'm thrown away, I'll turn into nothing but harmless dust in the ground. Just imagine if all plastic was like me. Pollution would be a thing of the past!

● Bioplastics are made from an oily chemical made by bacteria and plants
● The first bioplastic was invented in 1926
● Using bioplastic would cut down on litter by 90%

Biodegradable Plastic

Ocean Cleanup

■ Pollution Police

✳ This floating cleaner aims to rid oceans of plastics
✳ Will sweep up garbage to make waters pollution free
✳ Works day and night with no engine needed

Ahoy there! I'm about to set sail on a voyage of tidying up. An ocean-going plastic collector, I'll scoop up all the trash drifting in the ocean. I'm a free floater with a wide boom curving out on both sides. As the ocean currents and winds push me around, my boom sweeps any plastics into a container. I'm designed to work alone; no crew needed (or sails for that matter).

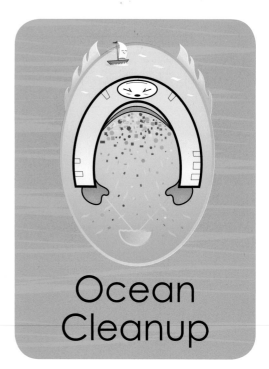

Ocean Cleanup

● The first Ocean Cleanup system was tested in the Pacific in 2019
● 10 million tons of plastic are dumped in the ocean each year
● In 2020, the first river-mouth system was launched to stop plastic reaching the ocean

Agrorobot
Pollution Police

✳ This mechatronic farmhand tends to crops
✳ Good for making food healthy, tasty, and less expensive
✳ Reduces need for chemicals such as fertilizers and pesticides

Agrorobot

My high-tech approach will bring much needed precision to farming. I can patrol the field using a leaf-recognition system to target tiny squirts of fertilizer on the crops that need it, while using a killer spray on any weeds that I spot on the way. My laser eye will scan fruit colors to check when they are ripe enough for harvest. And you can even leave the picking to me, too.

● Agrorobots will help grow food for the world's rising population
● Robots are being used to milk cows and shear sheep in place of humans
● A driverless electric tractor was launched in 2019

Waste Incinerator
■ Pollution Police

✳ A sparky fellow that turns waste into power
✳ Deals with trash that would otherwise be buried
✳ This pollution buster cleans up your act

Bring me your trash! I won't bury it—that just makes future pollution. No, I'll put it to work as a fuel, burning it away to make electricity. I use high temperatures to turn waste into simple gases and specks of ash. I filter poisons out to make them safe. And I have an electric field that zaps ash out of the hot gas. I make almost no smoke at all while I work. I like to keep things clean.

Waste Incinerator

● The world's biggest waste incinerator in Shanghai burns 6,600 tons a day
● Amager Hill, Copenhagen, hides a waste incinerator beneath a dry ski slope
● Making electricity from waste is expensive; let's make less waste in the first place

Catalytic Converter
Pollution Police ■

✳ Uses a team of chemical coworkers to filter filth
✳ Cleans the poisons coming from cars
✳ Improves air quality but cannot tackle greenhouse gases

Catalytic Converter

A senior member of this team, I'm under every car that burns a fuel to drive its engine. All sooty exhaust gases have to pass through me. I'm hollow but fitted with a fine metal mesh covered in tiny amounts of precious metals. These are my catalysts (chemical helpers). They convert poisons in the exhaust into safer stuff. Sadly, carbon dioxide goes straight through. I can't cut that!

● All gas and diesel cars have catalytic converters now; they were first used in 1973
● Uses platinum, palladium, and rhodium metals to make exhaust gases safer
● Electric cars do not use catalytic converters

Glossary

Artificial intelligence A computer system that can make decisions independent of a human controller.

Chemical reactor A safe place for chemicals to react, where they can mix up and then catch fire, explode, or give off poisons.

Eco-friendly Something that is kind to wildlife and the environment as a whole.

Fossil fuel Fuel, such as coal, natural gas, or oil, that is made from the remains of long-dead life-forms.

Generator A machine that creates electricity, usually by spinning magnets very fast.

Gigawatt A billion watts, where the watt is a measure of power. One watt (1 W) is needed to lift an apple up 3.3 feet (1 m) in one second.

Greenhouse gases Gases in the air that trap heat in the atmosphere. They work like a blanket to keep Earth warm. Too many of them will make Earth get too hot too quickly.

Hydrogen A gas that burns very easily and makes no smoke or pollution, just hot steam. Hydrogen might be a useful clean fuel in the future.

Infrared radiation Another term for heat. Infrared radiation is invisible, but we can feel it as warmth.

Lagoon A lake that is connected to the sea.

Magma Hot liquid rock that makes up some of the deep layers inside Earth. When the magma escapes and reaches Earth's surface, it is called lava.

Microbes Tiny life-forms, such as bacteria, that are too small to see without a microscope.

Photosynthesis A chemical process, carried out by trees and plants, that uses the energy in sunlight to create sugary food from carbon dioxide and water.

Polymer A long chemical made by chaining smaller chemicals together.

Radioactive When a substance has atoms that are unstable. The atoms fall apart, giving off energy.

Renewable energy A kind of energy that will never run out.

Sustainable A way of doing something that does not use up raw ingredients or other resources.

Turbine A fan-like machine that catches the flow of water, air, or other gases and converts that motion into a fast spin. Turbines are often used to spin generators (see above).

Ultraviolet light An invisible form of sunlight that can cause sunburn.

Index

Main entry in **bold**

A
Agrorobot **59**
Air Energy Storage **38**
Artificial Photosynthesis **42**

B
Biodegradable Plastic **56**
Biofuel **18**

C
Carbon Capture 28, **48**
Catalytic Converter **61**
Concentrated Solar **10**, 28

E
Electric Car **24**, 36, 61
Energy Vault 28, **40**

F
Fuel Cell **17**

G
Geoengineering **50**
Geothermal Power **14**

H
Hydroelectricity **20**, 22
Hyperloop 28, **44**

N
Nuclear Energy **16**
Nuclear Fusion 28, **43**

O
Ocean Cleanup **58**

P
Power Tower **32**
Pumped Storage **22**, 32

R
Recycling Machine **54**
Rewilding **26**

S
Smart Grid **36**, 40
Solar Panel **8**, 10, 22, 34, 35, 36, 42,
Spaceplane **46**
Storage Battery **35**, 36
Sustainability 4, 36, 63

T
Telepresence Robot **47**
Thermovoltaics **34**
Tidal Lagoon **30**

V
Vertical Farm **41**

W
Waste Incinerator **60**
Wind Turbine **12**, 22, 35